PIANO • VOCAL • GUITAR

Popular Songs from MOVIE SOUNDTRACKS

ISBN 978-1-4950-2262-3

HAL•LEONARD®
CORPORATION

7777 W. BLUEMOUND RD. P.O. BOX 13819 MILWAUKEE, WI 53213

Visit Hal Leonard Online at
www.halleonard.com

CONTENTS

AIN'T THAT A KICK IN THE HEAD

featured in A BRONX TALE

Words by SAMMY CAHN
Music by JAMES VAN HEUSEN

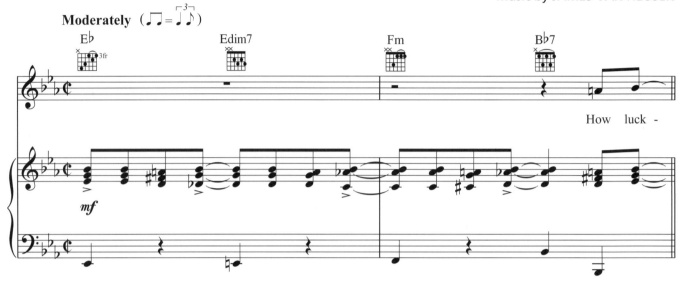

How luck-

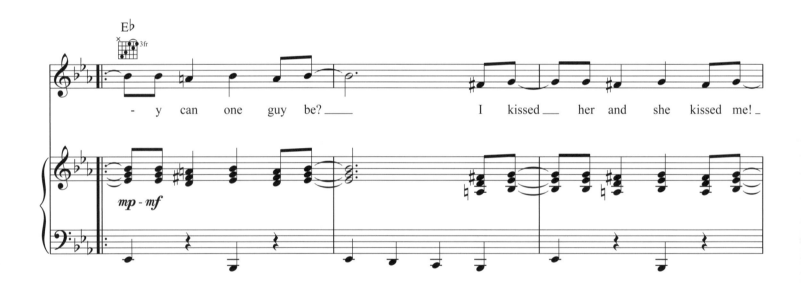

-y can one guy be? ___ I kissed ___ her and she kissed me! ___

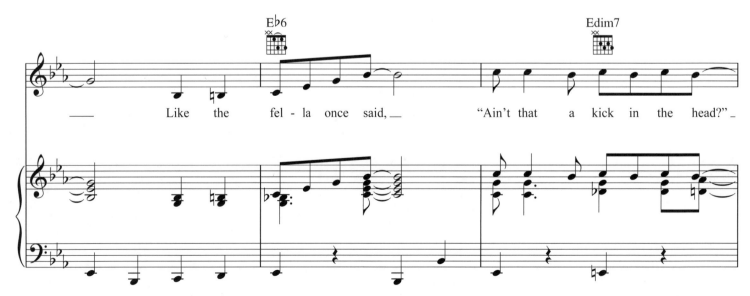

___ Like the fel-la once said, ___ "Ain't that a kick in the head?"

ALL BY MYSELF
featured in TO DIE FOR

Music by SERGEI RACHMANINOFF
Words and Additional Music by ERIC CARMEN

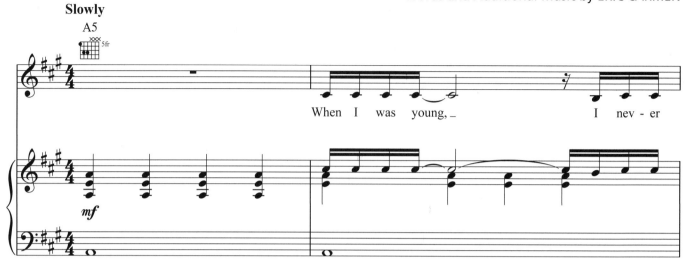

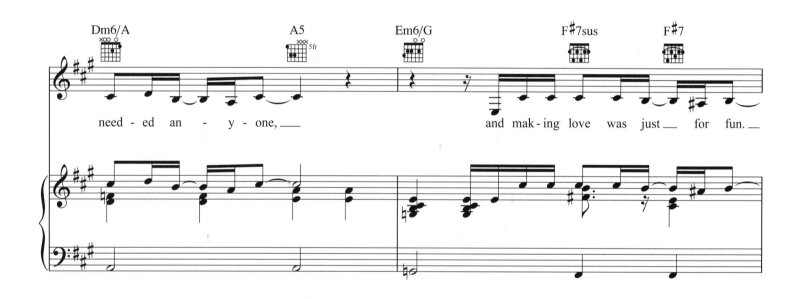

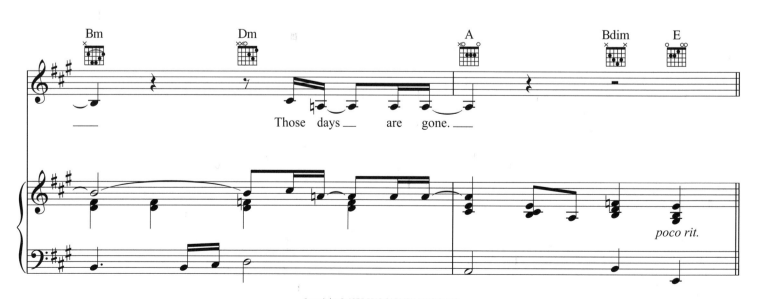

ALL I WANT IS YOU

featured in JUNO

Words and Music by
BARRY POLISAR

Moderately, in 2

If I was a flow-er grow-in' wild and free, all I'd want is you to be __ my

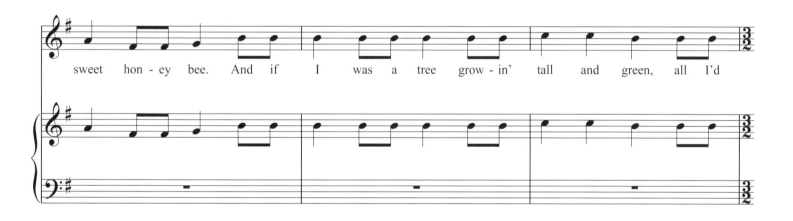

sweet hon-ey bee. And if I was a tree grow-in' tall and green, all I'd

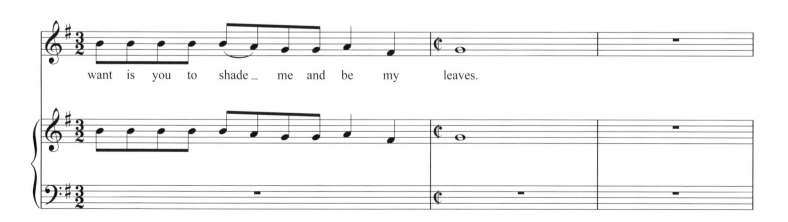

want is you to shade __ me and be my leaves.

If you were a riv-er in the
you were a wink, ____

moun-tains tall, the rum-ble of your wat-er would be my call. If
I'd be a nod. If you ___ were a seed, ___ well I'd be a pod. If

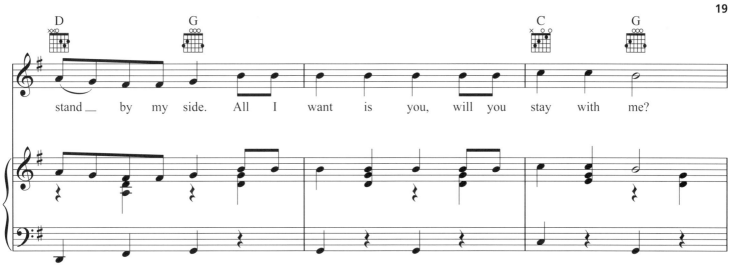

stand __ by my side. All I want is you, will you stay with me?

Hold me in your arms __ and sway me like the sea.

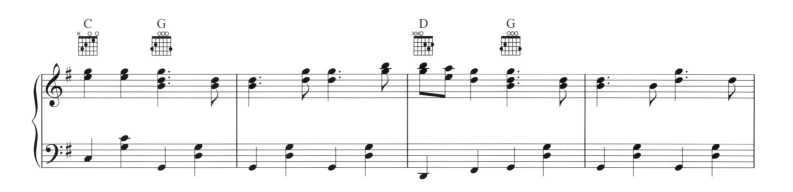

Repeat and Fade

Optional Ending

AMERICAN GIRL

featured in SILENCE OF THE LAMBS

Words and Music by
TOM PETTY

Moderately fast Rock

eas - y, ba - by,   make it last all night.
(Make it last all night.)

She was   an A - mer - i - can girl. _____

BABY, NOW THAT I'VE FOUND YOU

featured in SHALLOW HAL

Words and Music by TONY MACAULEY
and JOHN MacLEOD

AS TIME GOES BY
from CASABLANCA

Words and Music by
HERMAN HUPFELD

BABY, IT'S COLD OUTSIDE

featured in ELF

By FRANK LOESSER

BLACK BETTY
featured in BLOW

New words and new music adaptation by
HUDDIE LEDBETTER

BLAZE OF GLORY

featured in the film YOUNG GUNS II

Words and Music by
JON BON JOVI

Moderate Rock

wake up   in   the morn - ing and I   raise my wea - ry head, ____ I've got an
night I go to bed,   I pray the Lord my soul   to keep. _ No, I ain't

no one's son. Call me young gun.
dev-il's son. Call me young gun.

You

gun.

Guitar solo ad lib.

Play 3 times

Solo ends

BORN TO BE WILD

from EASY RIDER

Words and Music by
MARS BONFIRE

Moderate Rock

(1., 3.) Get your mo-tor run-ning. _____ Head out on the high - way _____

(2.) I like smoke and light - ning, _____ heav-y met-al thun-der _____

look-ing for ad-ven-ture in what

rac-ing in the wind and the

ev - er comes our way. _____

feel - ing that I'm un - der. _____

Yeah, dar-ling, gon-na

BRAND NEW KEY

featured in BOOGIE NIGHTS

Words and Music by
MELANIE SAFKA

get to - geth - er and try them out, __ you see. __

I been look - ing a - round a - while, __ you got some - thing for

me.   Oh, I got a brand new pair of roll - er skates,

you got a brand new key. __   key.

BUILD ME UP, BUTTERCUP

featured in THERE'S SOMETHING ABOUT MARY

Words and Music by TONY MACAULEY
and MICHAEL D'ABO

CALL ME

from the Paramount Motion Picture AMERICAN GIGOLO

Words by DEBORAH HARRY
Music by GIORGIO MORODER

DANGER ZONE
from the Motion Picture TOP GUN

Words and Music by GIORGIO MORODER
and TOM WHITLOCK

Rev - in' up your en - gine; lis - ten to her howl - in' roar. _____
Head - in' in the twi - light spread - in' out her wings to - night. _____
Out a - long the edge is al - ways where I burn to be. _____

Repeat and Fade

CAN'T HELP FALLING IN LOVE

from the Paramount Picture BLUE HAWAII

Words and Music by GEORGE DAVID WEISS,
HUGO PERETTI and LUIGI CREATORE

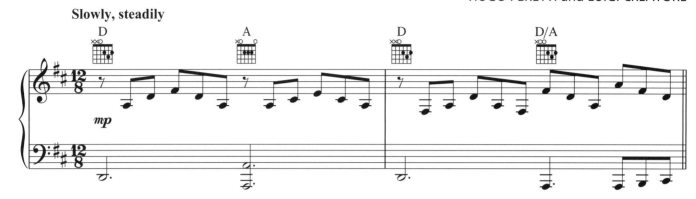

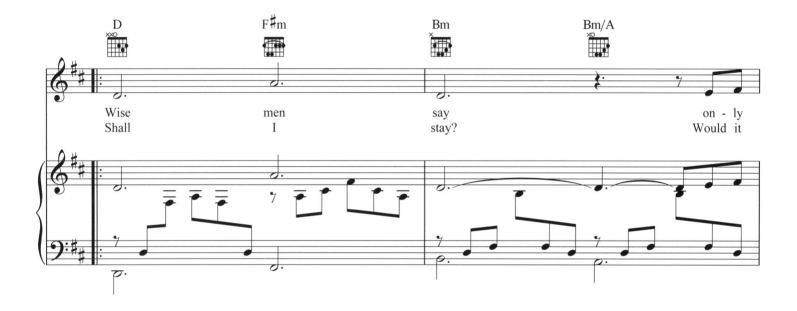

Wise   men   say   on - ly
Shall   I   stay?   Would it

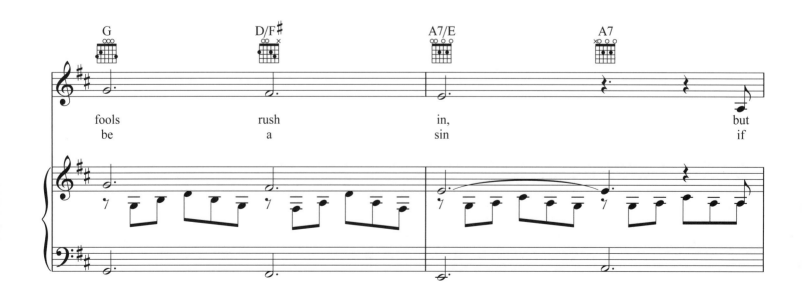

fools   rush   in,   but
be   a   sin   if

DON'T BE SHY
featured in HAROLD AND MAUDE

Words and Music by
CAT STEVENS

*Recorded a half step lower.

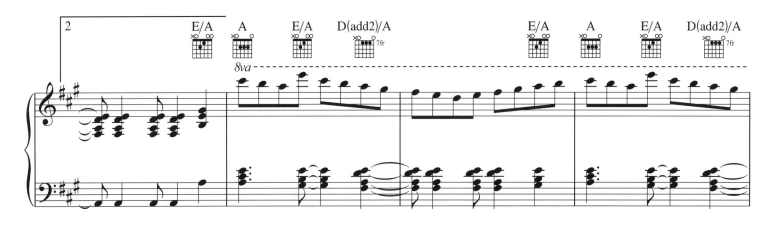

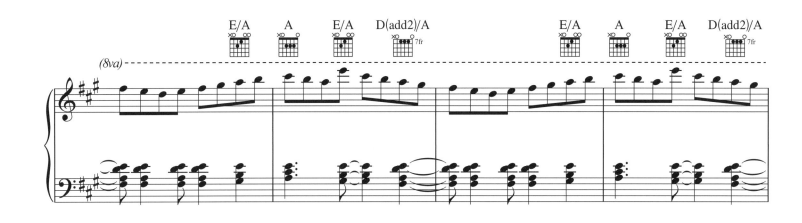

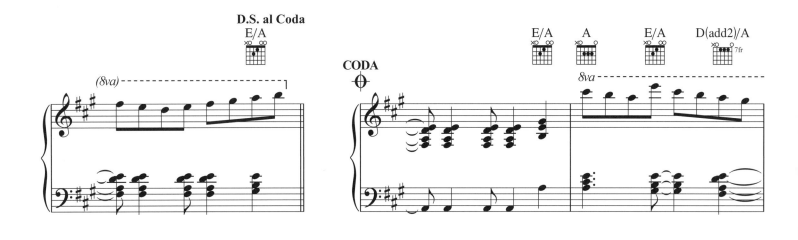

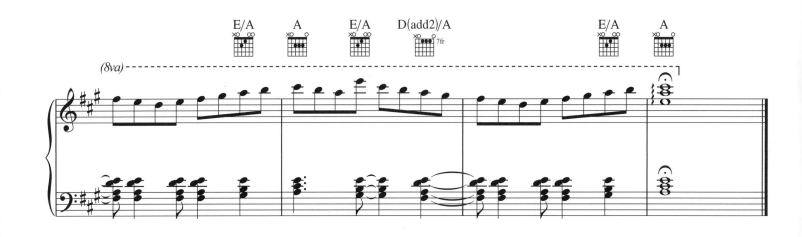

(Everything I Do)
I DO IT FOR YOU

from the Motion Picture ROBIN HOOD: PRINCE OF THIEVES

Words and Music by BRYAN ADAMS,
R.J. LANGE and MICHAEL KAMEN

Look in-to my eyes, _____
Look in-to your heart, _____

you will see _____ what you mean to _____ me.
you will find _____ there's noth - ing there to _____ hide.

Search your
Take me as I

heart, _____ search your soul, _____ and when you
am, _____ take my life, _____ I would

DON'T YOU
(Forget About Me)
from the Universal Picture THE BREAKFAST CLUB

Words and Music by KEITH FORSEY
and STEVE SCHIFF

END OF THE ROAD
from the Paramount Motion Picture BOOMERANG

Words and Music by BABYFACE,
L.A. REID and DARYL SIMMONS

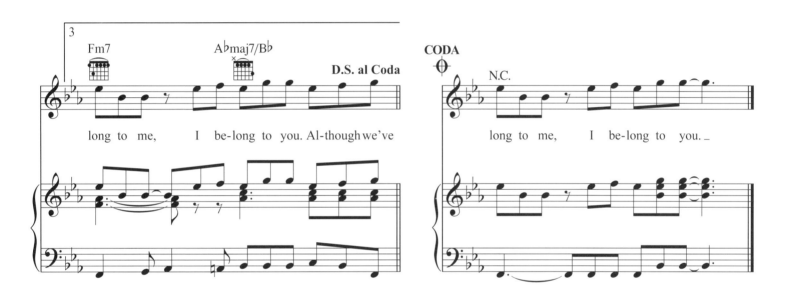

Additional Lyrics

(Spoken:) *Girl, I'm here for you.*
All those times at night when you just hurt me,
And just ran out with that other fellow,
Baby, I knew about it.
I just didn't care.
You just don't understand how much I love you, do you?
I'm here for you.
I'm not out to go out there and cheat all night just like you did, baby.
But that's alright, huh, I love you anyway.
And I'm still gonna be here for you 'til my dyin' day, baby.
Right now, I'm just in so much pain, baby.
'Cause you just won't come back to me, will you?
Just come back to me.

Yes, baby, my heart is lonely.
My heart hurts, baby, yes, I feel pain too.
Baby, please...

EYES OPEN
from THE HUNGER GAMES

Words and Music by
TAYLOR SWIFT

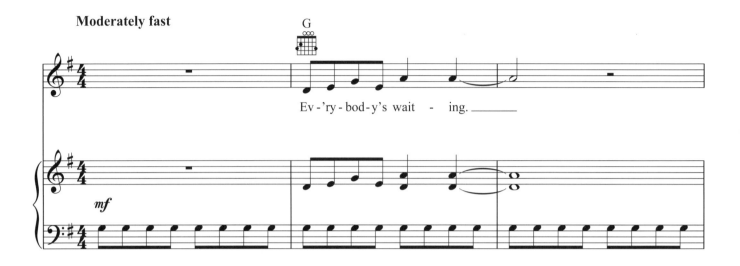

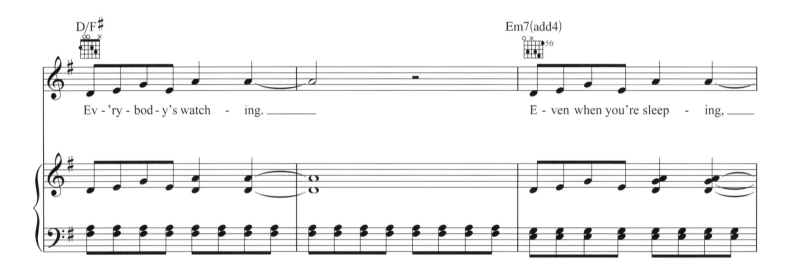

FREE BIRD
featured in THE DEVIL'S REJECTS

Words and Music by ALLEN COLLINS
and RONNIE VAN ZANT

HEY YOU

featured in THE SQUID AND THE WHALE

Words and Music by
ROGER WATERS

Hey you!

Out there in the cold, get-ting lone-ly, get-ting old, can you feel me? ___

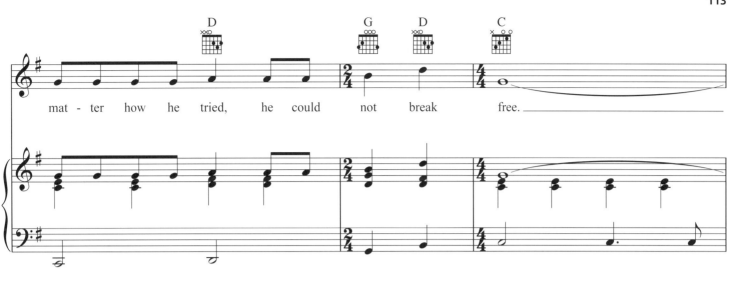

mat - ter how he tried, he could not break free. _____

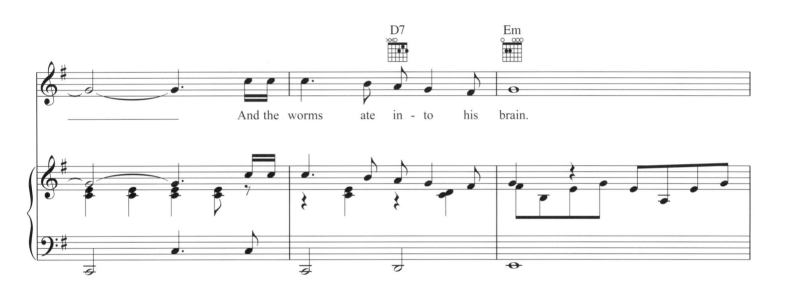

_____ And the worms ate in - to his brain.

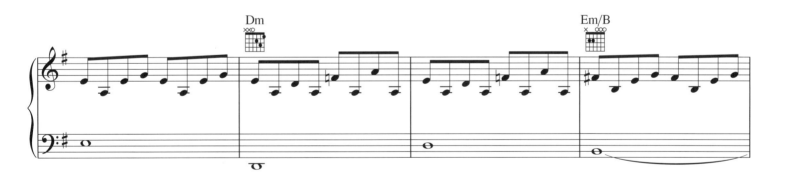

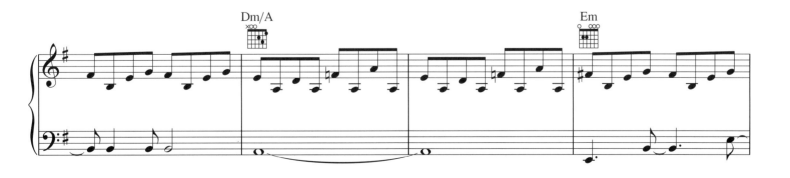

HIP TO BE SQUARE

featured in AMERICAN PSYCHO

Words and Music by BILL GIBSON,
SEAN HOPPER and HUEY LEWIS

HOLIDAY ROAD

featured in NATIONAL LAMPOON'S VACATION

Words and Music by
LINDSEY BUCKINGHAM

Fast Rock beat

Play 3 times

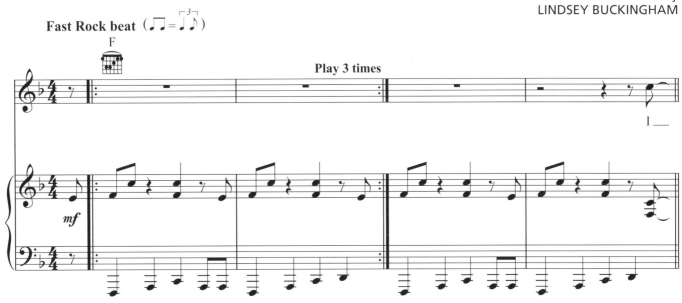

I ___

(1., D.S.) ___ found out ___ long ___ a - go ___ it's a long ___
(2.) ___ be nim - ble, Jack ___ be quick, ___ take ___

___ way down ___ the Hol - i - day Road. ___ Hol - i - day
___ a ride on the West Coast kick. ___

I BELIEVE I CAN FLY

from SPACE JAM

Words and Music by
ROBERT KELLY

I DON'T WANT TO MISS A THING

from the Touchstone Picture ARMAGEDDON

Words and Music by
DIANE WARREN

'Coz e-ven when I dream of you, the sweet-est dream would nev-er do. I'd still

miss you, ba-by, and I don't wan-na miss a thing. *(Vocal 1st time only)*

Repeat ad lib. and Fade

I GOT YOU BABE

featured in GROUNDHOG DAY

Words and Music by
SONNY BONO

you got me, and ba - by, I got you,

babe, I got you, babe. I got

you, babe. They say our love won't pay the rent. Be -

I HEARD IT THROUGH THE GRAPEVINE

featured in THE BIG CHILL

Words and Music by NORMAN J. WHITFIELD
and BARRETT STRONG

D.S. al Coda

Peo - ple say be - lieve half ___

CODA

___ yeah, yeah, ___ yeah. I heard it through the grape - vine, not much

Repeat and Fade

long - er would you be mine, ba - by. Yeah, __

I JUST CALLED TO SAY I LOVE YOU

featured in THE WOMAN IN RED

Words and Music by
STEVIE WONDER

Chorus

Additional Lyrics

3. No summer's high; no warm July;
No harvest moon to light one tender August night.
No autumn breeze; no falling leaves;
Not even time for birds to fly to southern skies.

4. No Libra sun; no Halloween;
No giving thanks to all the Christmas joy you bring.
But what it is, though old so new
To fill your heart like no three words could ever do.
Chorus

I WANT YOU BACK

featured in GUARDIANS OF THE GALAXY

Words and Music by FREDDIE PERREN,
ALPHONSO MIZELL, BERRY GORDY JR.
and DEKE RICHARDS

I WILL ALWAYS LOVE YOU

featured in THE BODYGUARD

Words and Music by
DOLLY PARTON

* Recorded a half step higher.

I'M SHIPPING UP TO BOSTON

featured in THE DEPARTED

Words and Music by ALEXANDER BARR,
KEN CASEY, WOODY GUTHRIE
and MATTHEW KELLY

Lively Jig tempo

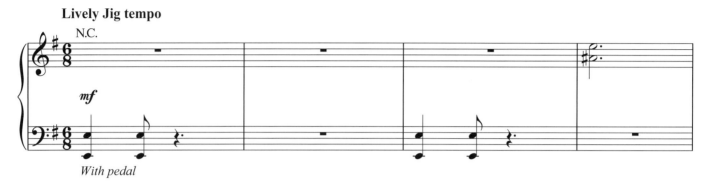

I'm ship - ping up _____ to Bos - ton, _____

(I've Had)
THE TIME OF MY LIFE
from DIRTY DANCING

Words and Music by FRANKE PREVITE,
JOHN DeNICOLA and DONALD MARKOWITZ

Male: Now I've had the time of my life. ___ No, I

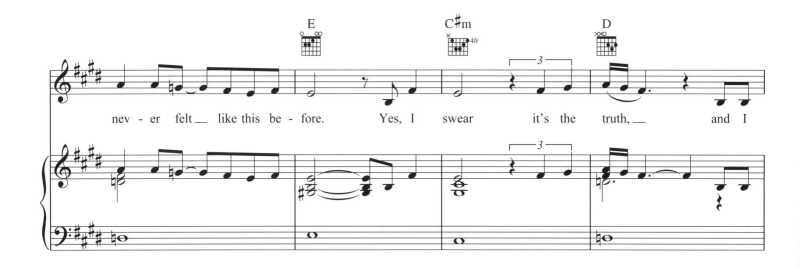

nev-er felt ___ like this be-fore. Yes, I swear it's the truth, ___ and I

owe it all to you. ___ Female: 'Cause ___ I've had the time of my life, ___ and I

176

IF YOU WERE HERE

featured in SIXTEEN CANDLES

Words and Music by THOMAS BAILY,
ALANNAH CURRIE and JOSEPH LEEWAY

on - ly ___ to rise and ___ fall a - gain.

IT MIGHT BE YOU
Theme from TOOTSIE

Words by ALAN and MARILYN BERGMAN
Music by DAVE GRUSIN

Time: I've been pass-ing time __ watch-ing trains go by. __
— look-ing back as lov- ers go walk-ing past. __

LIFE IS A HIGHWAY
featured in CARS

Words and Music by
TOM COCHRANE

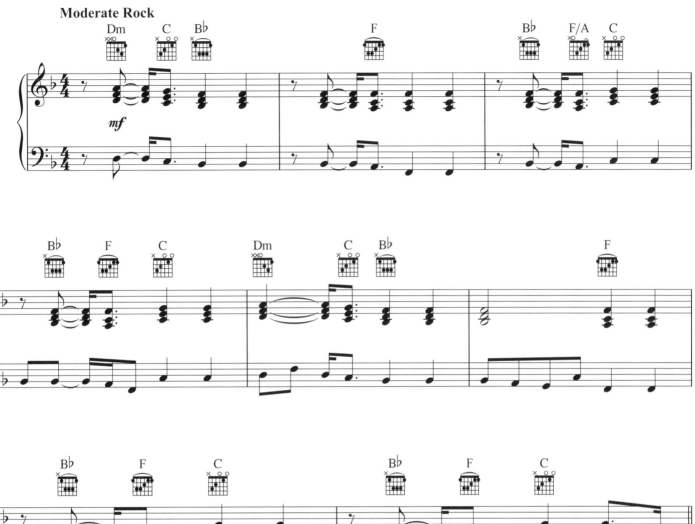

Life's like a road _ that you trav-el on when there's one __ day here _ and the next _ day gone. __ Some-times _
all these cit-ies and all these towns, it's in my blood _ and it's all __ a-round. _ I love _

IT MUST HAVE BEEN LOVE

featured in PRETTY WOMAN

Words and Music by
PER GESSLE

wind ___ blows. ___

JUST DROPPED IN
(To See What Condition My Condition Was In)
featured in THE BIG LEBOWSKI

Words and Music by
MICKEY NEWBURY

LONG BLACK ROAD

featured in AMERICAN HUSTLE

Words and Music by
JEFF LYNNE

long   black   road. _
long   black   road. _

You got - ta
You got - ta

Guitar solo ad lib.

(Solo ends)   Long   black   road. _

Repeat and Fade

Optional Ending

rit.

LOVE IS STRANGE

featured in DIRTY DANCING

By SYLVIA ROBINSON,
ETHEL SMITH and MICKEY BAKER

missed.

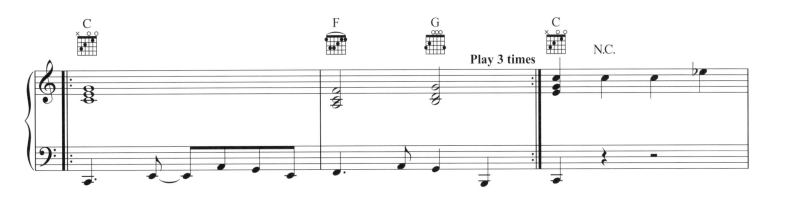

Play 3 times

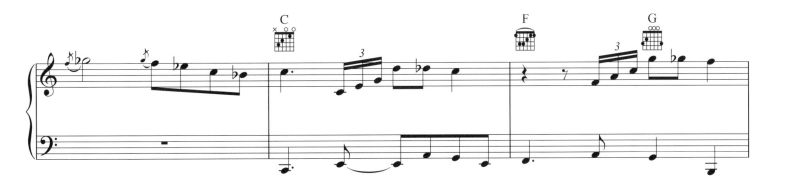

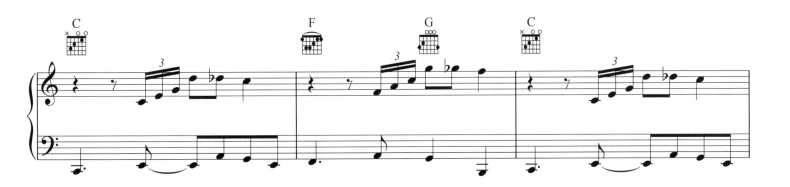

mm,   you're the   one.

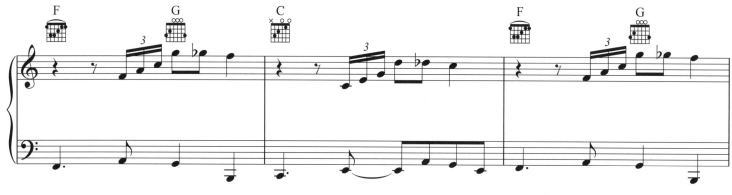

Repeat and Fade

Optional Ending

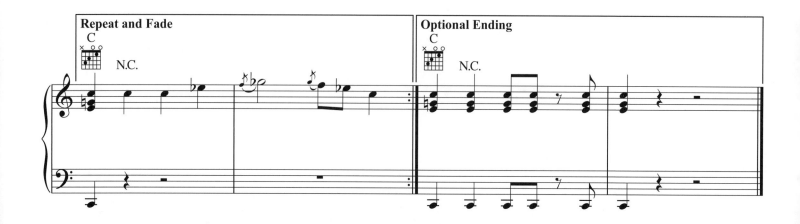

LOVE NEVER FELT SO GOOD

featured in XSCAPE

Words and Music by MICHAEL JACKSON
and PAUL ANKA

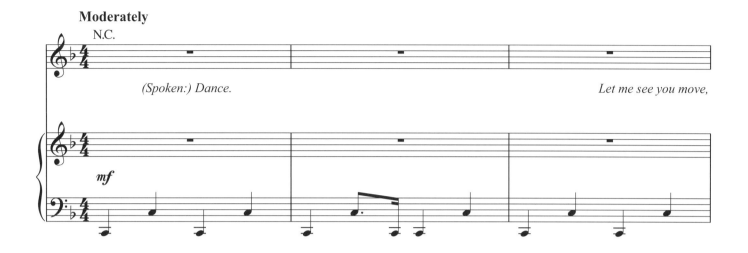

Moderately

(Spoken:) Dance.

Let me see you move,

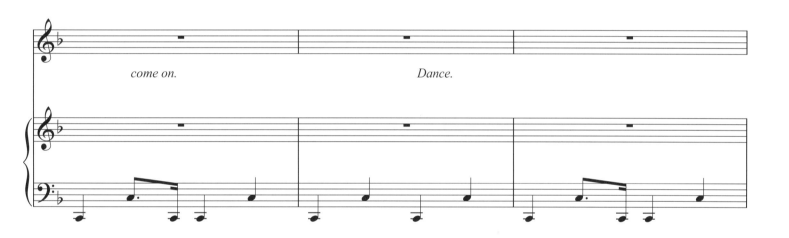

come on.

Dance.

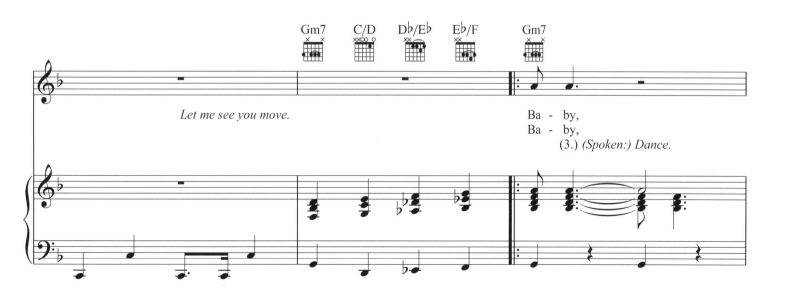

Gm7   C/D   Db/Eb   Eb/F   Gm7

Let me see you move.

Ba - by,
Ba - by,
(3.) (Spoken:) Dance.

MIDNIGHT RIDER

featured in THE DEVIL'S REJECTS

Words and Music by GREGG ALLMAN
and ROBERT KIM PAYNE

Moderate Southern Rock

And I've got to

run _____ to keep _____ from hid-in'. And I'm
own _____ the clothes _____ I'm wear-in'. And the
past _____ the point _____ of car-in'. Same ol'

bound _____ to keep _____ on rid-in'.
road _____ goes on _____ for-ev-er.
bed _____ I'll soon _____ be shar-in'.

And I've _____ got

MUSTANG SALLY

featured in THE COMMITMENTS

Words and Music by
BONNY RICE

Mus - tang Sal - ly, think you bet - ter slow your mus - tang down. Mus - tang

All you want to do is ride a- round, Sal - ly. Ride, Sal - ly, ride. ___

All you want to do is ride a- round, Sal - ly. Ride, Sal - ly, ride. ___

___ All you want to do is ride a- round, Sal - ly.

NOTHING'S GONNA STOP US NOW

featured in MANNEQUIN

Words and Music by DIANE WARREN
and ALBERT HAMMOND

OH, PRETTY WOMAN
featured in PRETTY WOMAN

Words and Music by ROY ORBISON
and BILL DEES

OLD TIME ROCK & ROLL
featured in RISKY BUSINESS

Words and Music by GEORGE JACKSON
and THOMAS E. JONES III

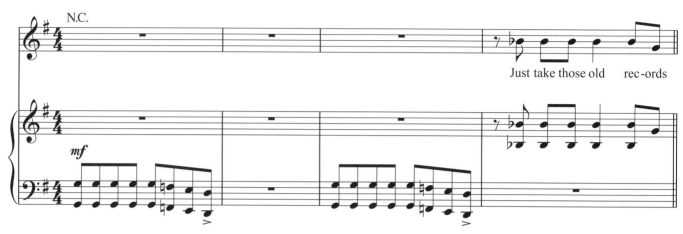

Moderate Rock 'n' Roll beat

Just take those old rec-ords

off the shelf. _ I'll sit and lis-ten to 'em by my-self. _

tan - go. _____ I'd rath-er hear some blues or funk-y old soul. _

To - day's mu - sic ain't got the same soul. I like that old - time _

There's on - ly one sure way to get me to go; start play - ing old - time _

soothes my soul. __ I rem - i - nisce a - bout the days of old __

with that old - time rock 'n' roll. __

N.C.

1. *Guitar solo ad lib.*
2. *Saxophone solo ad lib.*

(You've Got)
PERSONALITY

featured in THE HELP

Words and Music by LLOYD PRINCE
and HAROLD LOGAN

THE POWER OF LOVE

featured in BACK TO THE FUTURE

Words and Music by JOHNNY COLLA,
CHRIS HAYES and HUEY LEWIS

PRETTY THING
featured in WOLF OF WALL STREET

Words and Music by
WILLIE DIXON

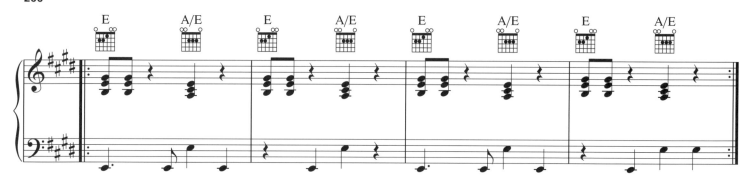

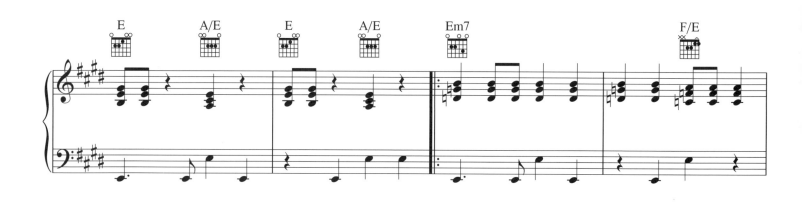

Harmonica solo ad lib.

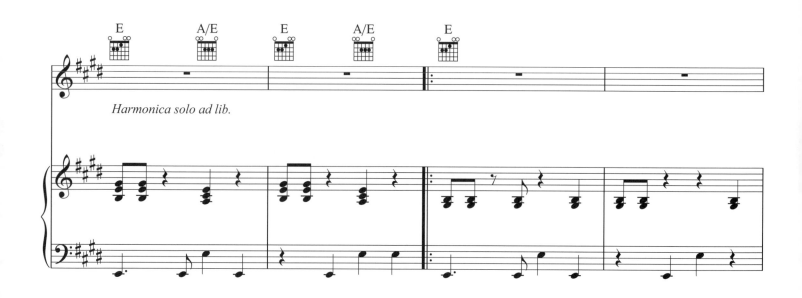

oh, _____ you pret - ty thing.

Harmonica fills ad lib. to end

Repeat and Fade

Optional Ending

SAY YOU, SAY ME
from the Motion Picture WHITE NIGHTS

Words and Music by
LIONEL RICHIE

lieve in who — you are; ____ you are a shin - ing star. ____

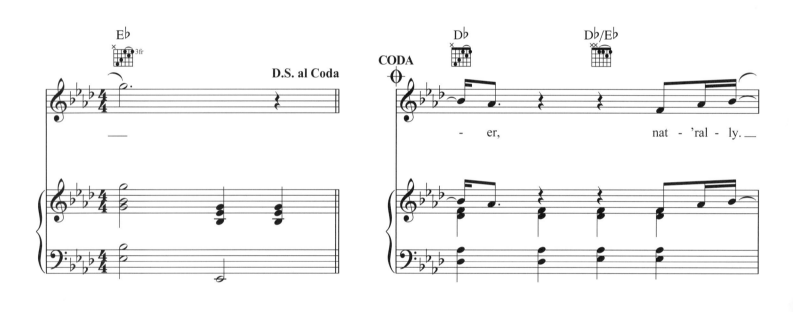

— er, nat - 'ral - ly. __

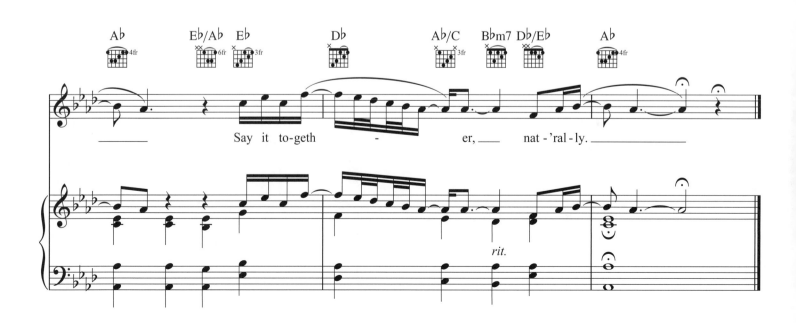

Say it to-geth - er, __ nat - 'ral-ly. ____

STUCK IN THE MIDDLE WITH YOU

featured in RESERVOIR DOGS

Words and Music by GERRY RAFFERTY
and JOE EGAN

Lyrics:

know why I came here to-night.

stuck in the mid-dle with you

Tryin' to make some sense of it all

I got the

and I'm won-

but I can see

(1.) Well, I don't

Instrumental

SENTIMENTAL JOURNEY

featured in FOUR ROOMS

Words and Music by BUD GREEN,
LES BROWN and BEN HOMER

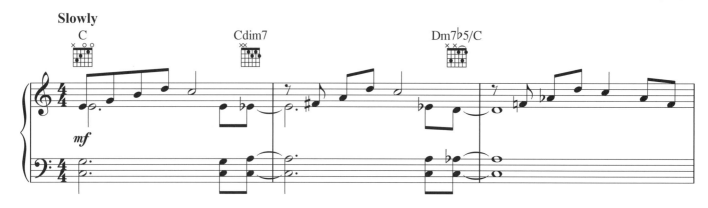

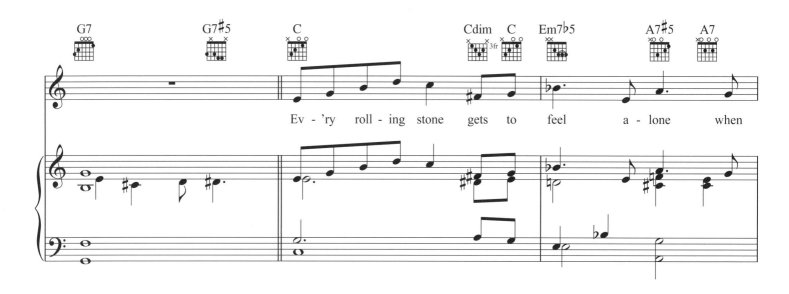

Ev - 'ry roll - ing stone gets to feel a - lone when

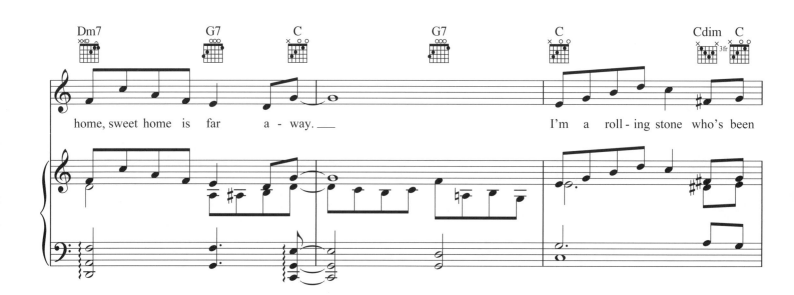

home, sweet home is far a - way. ___ I'm a roll - ing stone who's been

SHOUT

featured in NATIONAL LAMPOON'S ANIMAL HOUSE

Words and Music by O'KELLY ISLEY,
RONALD ISLEY and RUDOLPH ISLEY

SOMEBODY'S BABY

featured in FAST TIMES AT RIDGEMONT HIGH

Words and Music by DANNY KORTCHMAR
and JACKSON BROWNE

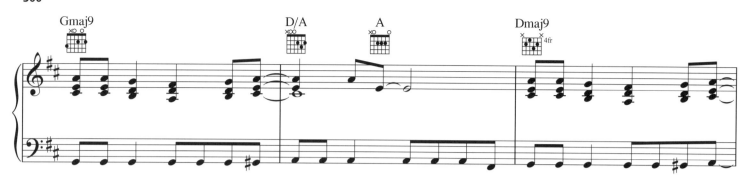

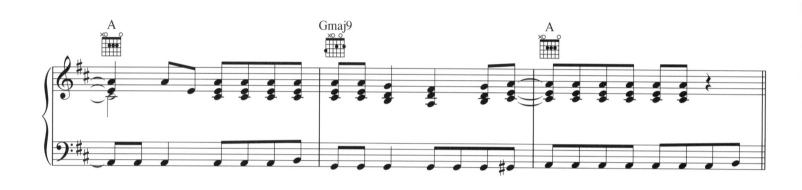

Yeah, she's gon-na be some-bod-y's on-ly light, gon-na

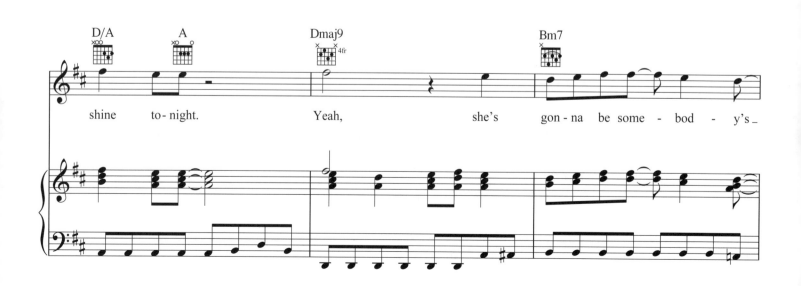

shine to-night. Yeah, she's gon-na be some-bod-y's_

SON-OF-A-PREACHER MAN
featured in PULP FICTION

Words and Music by JOHN HURLEY
and RONNIE WILKINS

SUMMER BREEZE

featured in DAZED & CONFUSED

Words and Music by JAMES SEALS
and DASH CROFTS

Lyrics:
See the cur-tains hang-in' in the win-dow ___ in the eve-ning on a Fri-day night. ___
See the pa-per lay-in' on the side-walk, ___ a lit-tle mu-sic from the house next door. ___

A lit-tle light a-shin-in' through the win-dow ___
So I walk on up to the door-step, ___

SUMMER IN THE CITY
featured in DIE HARD WITH A VENGEANCE

Words and Music by JOHN SEBASTIAN,
STEVE BOONE and MARK SEBASTIAN

Hot town, sum-mer in the cit-y, back o' my neck get-tin' dirt-y and grit-ty.
Cool town, eve-nin' in the cit-y, dressed so fine and a-look-in' so pret-ty.

Instrumental to Fade

Been down, is-n't it a pit-y? Does-n't seem to be a shad-ow in the cit-y.
Cool cat, look-in' for a kit-ty. Gon-na look in ev-'ry cor-ner of the cit-y.

All a-round, peo-ple look-in' half dead, walk-in' on the side-walk hot-ter than a match-head.
Till I'm wheez-in' like a bus stop, run-nin' up the stairs, gon-na meet you on the roof-top.

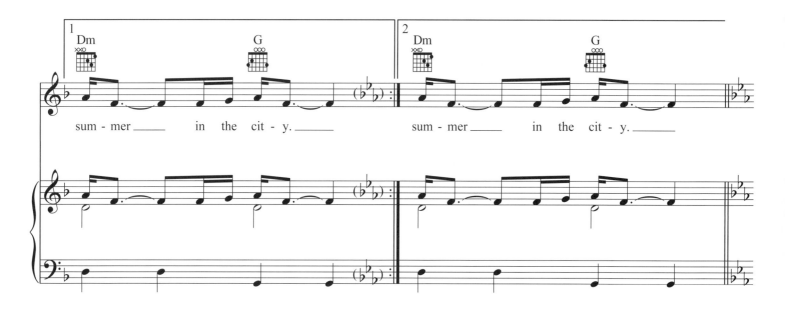

sum - mer _____ in the cit - y. _____   sum - mer _____ in the cit - y. _____

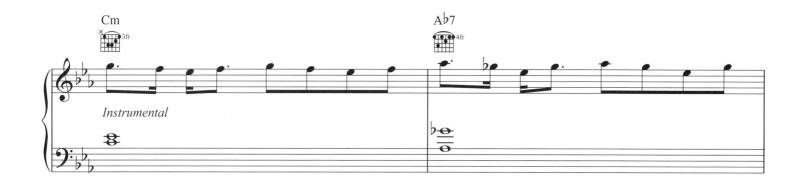

Instrumental

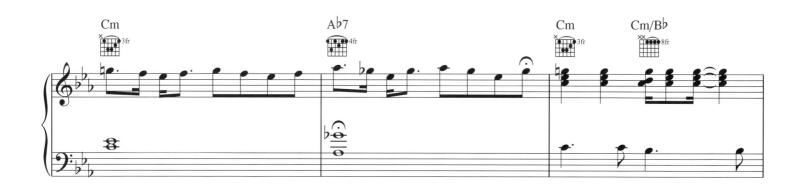

D.S. and Fade
(Instrumental)

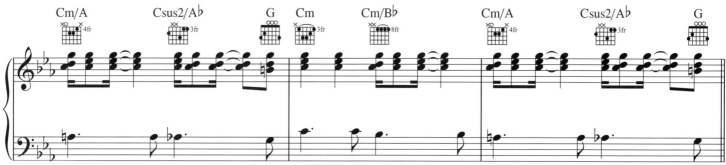

TROUBLE
featured in HAROLD AND MAUDE

Words and Music by
CAT STEVENS

Moderately fast, half-time feel

Trou-ble, _____ oh, trou-ble, set me free. _____
Trou-ble, _____ oh, trou-ble, move a-way. _____
Trou-ble, _____ oh, trou-ble, move from me. _____

I have seen your face and it's too much, too much for me. _____
I have seen your face and it's too much for me to-day. _____
I have paid my debt, now won't you leave me in my mis-er-y?

Trou-ble, _____ oh,
Trou-ble, _____ oh,
Trou-ble, _____ oh,

*Recorded a half step higher.

SUPERSTITION

featured in THE THING

Words and Music by
STEVIE WONDER

(1., 3.) Thir-teen month old ba-
(2.) Keep me in a day-

- by broke the look-ing glass.
- dream, keep me go-in' strong.

Sev - en years of bad
You don't wan - na save

luck. The good things in your past.
me. Sad is my song.

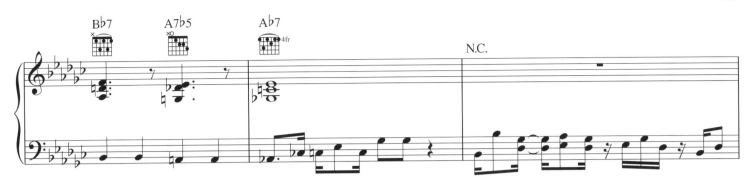

Ver - y su - per - sti -

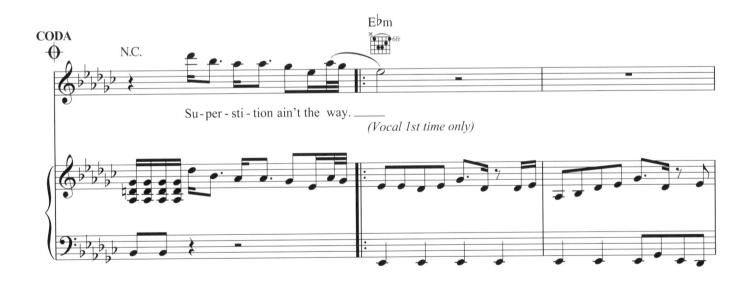

Su - per - sti - tion ain't the way. ____

(Vocal 1st time only)

Repeat and Fade

Optional Ending

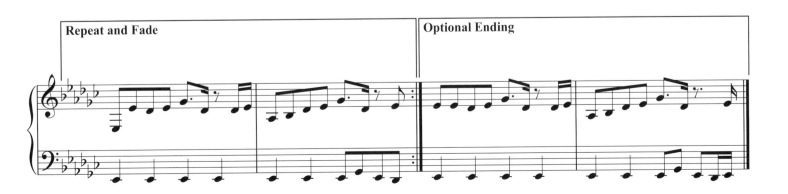

THINGS HAVE CHANGED

from WONDER BOYS

Words and Music by
BOB DYLAN

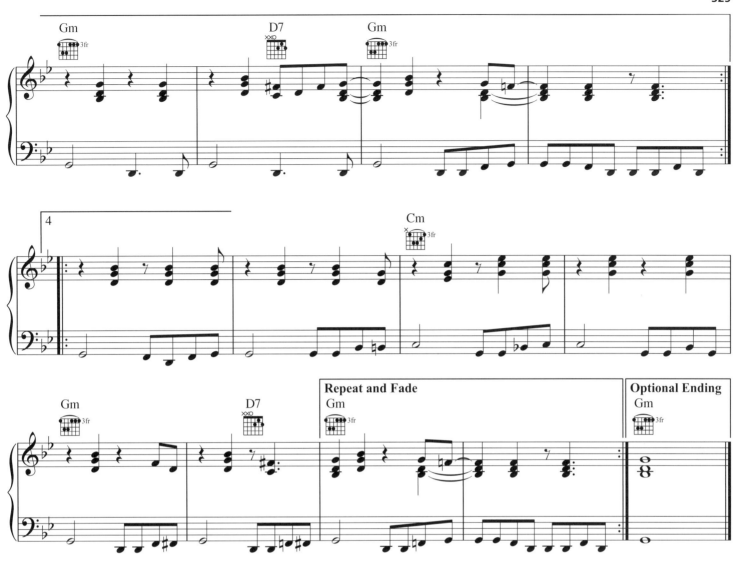

Additional Lyrics

2. This place ain't doin' me any good.
   I'm in the wrong town, I should be in Hollywood.
   Just for a second there I thought I saw something move.
   Gonna take dancing lessons, do the jitterbug rag.
   Ain't no shortcuts, gonna dress in drag.
   Only a fool in here would think he's got anything to prove.
   Lot of water under the bridge, lot of other stuff too.
   Don't get up gentlemen, I'm only passing through.
   Chorus

3. I've been walking forty miles of bad road.
   If the Bible is right, the world will explode.
   I've been trying to get as far away from myself as I can.
   Some things are too hot to touch.
   The human mind can only stand so much.
   You can't win with a losing hand.
   Feel like falling in love with the first woman I meet,
   Putting her in a wheelbarrow and wheeling her down the street.
   Chorus

4. I hurt easy, I just don't show it.
   You can hurt someone and not even know it.
   The next sixty seconds could be like an eternity.
   Gonna get low down, gonna fly high.
   All the truth in the world adds up to one big lie.
   I'm in love with a woman who don't even appeal to me.
   Mr. Jinx and Miss Lucy, they jumped in the lake.
   I'm not that eager to make a mistake.
   Chorus

THIS WOMAN'S WORK
from SHE'S HAVING A BABY

Words and Music by
KATE BUSH

*Male vocal written at pitch.

A THOUSAND YEARS

from the Summit Entertainment film THE TWILIGHT SAGA: BREAKING DAWN – PART 1

Words and Music by DAVID HODGES
and CHRISTINA PERRI

I'll love you for ___ a thou - sand more.

TWIST AND SHOUT

featured in FERRIS BUELLER'S DAY OFF

Words and Music by BERT RUSSELL
and PHIL MEDLEY

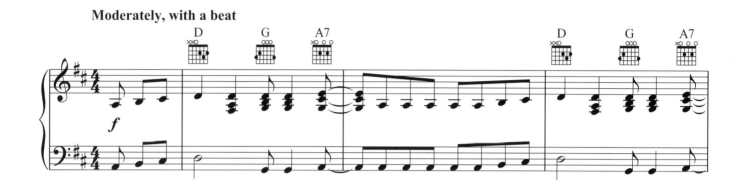

Well, shake it up, ba - by, __ now,
- by, __ now, (Shake it up, ba - by) Twist and
- by, __ now,

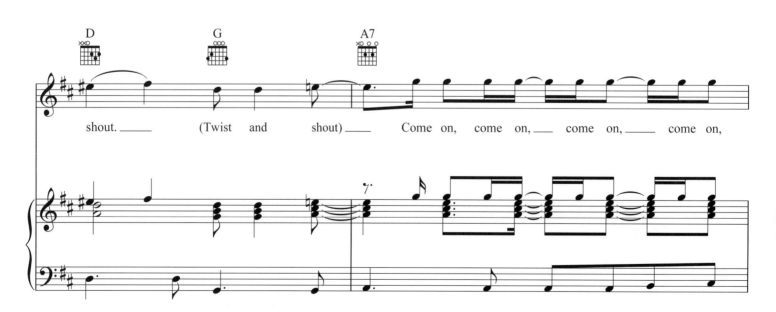

shout. ___ (Twist and shout) ___ Come on, come on, __ come on, __ come on,

UNCHAINED MELODY

featured in the Motion Picture GHOST

Lyric by HY ZARET
Music by ALEX NORTH

WAITING FOR SOMEBODY
featured in SINGLES

Words and Music by
PAUL WESTERBERG

wait-ing for __ some-bod - y all my life.
(Ah, ha, ha.)

Guitar solo to end (Hey!) (Hey!)

(Hey!)

Repeat and Fade

Optional Ending

WALKING ON SUNSHINE
featured in HIGH FIDELITY

Written by KIMBERLEY REW

Bright Rock

WHAT THE WORLD NEEDS NOW IS LOVE

featured in MY BEST FRIEND'S WEDDING

Lyric by HAL DAVID
Music by BURT BACHARACH

With a Jazz Waltz feel

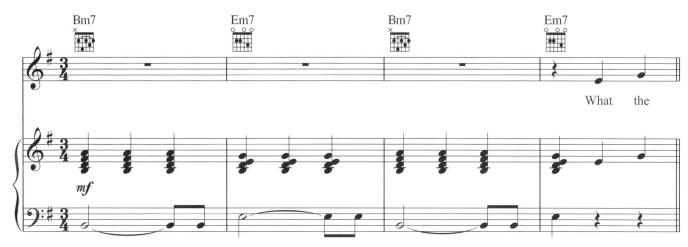

WHITE RABBIT

featured in FEAR AND LOATHING IN LAS VEGAS

Words and Music by
GRACE SLICK

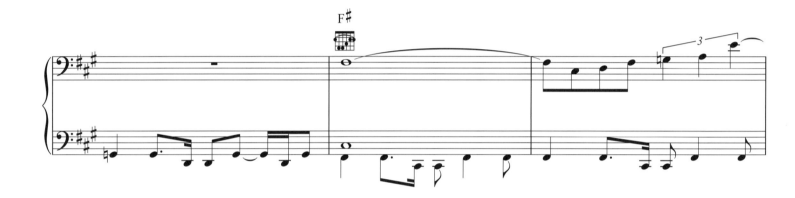

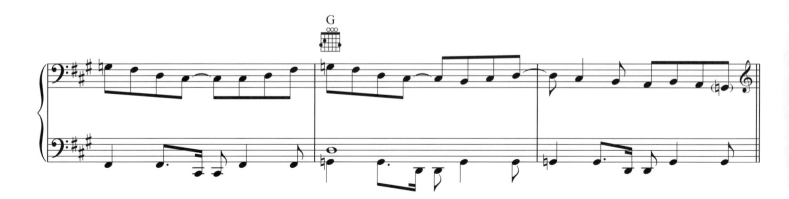

Psychedelic Stomp

WISE UP
featured in MAGNOLIA

Words and Music by
AIMEE MANN

YOUNG AND BEAUTIFUL
from THE GREAT GATSBY

Words and Music by RICK NOWELS
and ELIZABETH GRANT

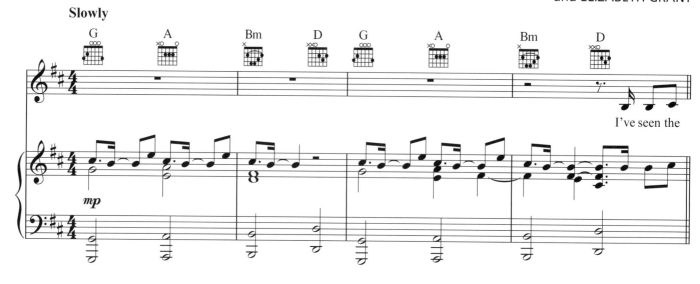

I've seen the

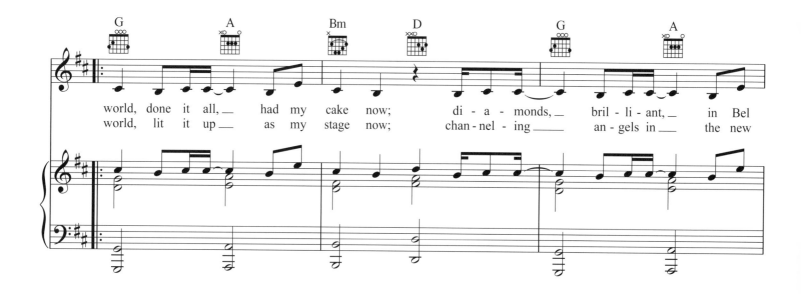

world, done it all, ___ had my cake now; ___ di - a - monds, ___ bril - li - ant, ___ in Bel -
world, lit it up ___ as my stage now; ___ chan - nel - ing ___ an - gels in ___ the new

Air now. Hot sum - mer nights, ___ mid - Ju - ly, ___ when you and I were for - ev - er wild. ___ The cra - zy
age now. Hot sum - mer days, ___ rock 'n' roll, ___ the way you play for me at your show; ___ and all the

THE BEST EVER COLLECTION
ARRANGED FOR PIANO, VOICE AND GUITAR

100 of the Most Beautiful Piano Solos Ever
100 songs
00102787 ....$27.50

150 of the Most Beautiful Songs Ever
150 ballads
00360735 ....$27.00

150 More of the Most Beautiful Songs Ever
150 songs
00311318 ....$29.99

More of the Best Acoustic Rock Songs Ever
69 tunes
00311738 ....$19.95

Best Acoustic Rock Songs Ever
65 acoustic hits
00310984 ....$19.95

Best Big Band Songs Ever
68 big band hits
00359129 ....$17.99

Best Blues Songs Ever
73 blues tunes
00312874 ....$19.99

Best Broadway Songs Ever
83 songs
00309155 ....$24.99

More of the Best Broadway Songs Ever
82 songs
00311501 ....$22.95

Best Children's Songs Ever
102 songs
00310358 ....$22.99

Best Christmas Songs Ever
69 holiday favorites
00359130 ....$24.99

Best Classic Rock Songs Ever
64 hits
00310800 ....$22.99

Best Classical Music Ever
86 classical favorites
00310674 (Piano Solo) $19.95

The Best Country Rock Songs Ever
52 hits
00118881 ....$19.99

Best Country Songs Ever
78 classic country hits
00359135 ....$19.99

Best Disco Songs Ever
50 songs
00312565 ....$19.99

Best Dixieland Songs Ever
90 songs
00312326 ....$19.99

Best Early Rock 'n' Roll Songs Ever
74 songs
00310816 ....$19.95

Best Easy Listening Songs Ever
75 mellow favorites
00359193 ....$19.99

Best Folk/Pop Songs Ever
66 hits
00138299 ....$19.99

Best Gospel Songs Ever
80 gospel songs
00310503 ....$19.99

Best Hymns Ever
118 hymns
00310774 ....$18.99

Best Jazz Piano Solos Ever
80 songs
00312079 ....$19.99

Best Jazz Standards Ever
77 jazz hits
00311641 ....$19.95

More of the Best Jazz Standards Ever
74 beloved jazz hits
00311023 ....$19.95

Best Latin Songs Ever
67 songs
00310355 ....$19.99

Best Love Songs Ever
62 favorite love songs
00359198 ....$19.99

Best Movie Songs Ever
71 songs
00310063 ....$19.99

Best Movie Soundtrack Songs Ever
70 songs
00146161 ....$16.99

Best Pop/Rock Songs Ever
50 classics
00138279 ....$19.99

Best Praise & Worship Songs Ever
80 all-time favorites
00311057 ....$22.99

More of the Best Praise & Worship Songs Ever
76 songs
00311800 ....$24.99

Best R&B Songs Ever
66 songs
00310184 ....$19.95

Best Rock Songs Ever
63 songs
00490424 ....$18.95

Best Showtunes Ever
71 songs
00118782 ....$19.99

Best Songs Ever
72 must-own classics
00359224 ....$24.99

Best Soul Songs Ever
70 hits
00311427 ....$19.95

Best Standards Ever, Vol. 1 (A-L)
72 beautiful ballads
00359231 ....$17.95

Best Standards Ever, Vol. 2 (M-Z)
73 songs
00359232 ....$17.99

Best Torch Songs Ever
70 sad and sultry favorites
00311027 ....$19.95

Best Wedding Songs Ever
70 songs
00311096 ....$19.95

Visit us online
for complete songlists at
www.halleonard.com

HAL•LEONARD® CORPORATION
7777 W. BLUEMOUND RD. P.O. BOX 13819 MILWAUKEE, WI 53213

0516